Cats and Dogs in Space

Speculative Poetry About our Feline Friends and Canine Companions

Lisa Timpf

Cats and Dogs in Space
Lisa Timpf

All rights reserved. No part of this book may be reproduced or transmitted in any form or by any means, electronic or mechanical, including photocopying or recording or by any information storage and retrieval systems, without expressed written consent of the author and/or artists.

Cats and Dogs in Space is a work of fiction. Names, characters, places, and incidents are products of the author's imagination. Any resemblance to actual events or persons, living or dead, is entirely coincidental.

Poem copyrights owned by Lisa Timpf
Cover illustration and design by Marcia Borell
Interior Illustrations by t.santitoro

First Printing February 2025

Hiraeth Publishing
P.O. Box 1248
Alamogordo, NM 88310
e-mail: hiraethsubs@yahoo.com

Visit www.hiraethsffh.com for online science fiction, fantasy, horror, scifaiku, and more. Stop by our online Shop for novels, magazines, anthologies, and collections. **Support the small, independent press...and your First Amendment rights.**

Cats and Dogs in Space:
Speculative Poetry About our Feline Friends
and Canine Companions
is dedicated to the feline and canine members
of my "fur family,"
who have all offered love, companionship,
and moments of amusement,
regardless of how long or short a time
they stayed with us.

For Patsy, Mickey, Tiny, Sneeks, Jak,
Emma, Boomer, Smokey, Lola,
and Chet.

Table of Contents

7   From the Headlines: Poems Sparked by News Stories
Cryptic
The Truth is Out
Hanging Them Up
Chaser Checks Out
Lost and Found
Military Ghost Dog
For Laika
The Cats Have Their Say
Canem Roboto

19   Legendary: Riffing on Myth, Legend, and Folklore
From Cat to Fiddle
Nursery Rhymes for Changing Times
What *Really* Happened
Thoughts on Cerberus
Musings of a Shelter Dog
The Last Dog

27   The Great Hereafter
The Cat's Message
To Let You Go Gently
Farewell To an Old Friend
The Only Enduring Thing
Paws for Reflection
Now You're Gone
Without Her
Herding the Stars
Over the Rainbow
Here/Not Here
The Unknown After
Ghostly Dog

This Tree
Ghost Train
Ghost Dogs at Play
[sunlight refracts]

45 Cats and Dogs of the Future
The Changing Face of Fear
The 22nd Century Guide to Purr-sonality Types
The Cats of the Future
Dogs of the 2080s
[canine deity]
[alternate reality]
Chimerapet
Canis Futuris
Dogs in Space
Fidelis Reinvented
When We Leave Home for Good
The Sand Dogs of Mars
Steampunk Paradise
A Cat's Confession
Separate and Apart
An Understanding
[what's got into *him*]
Unexpected
[a swim in Arcadia's murky river]
[playing fetch on Mars]

64 References for "From the Headlines" poems

66 Previous Appearances

69 Acknowledgements

70 About the Author

From the Headlines:
Poems Sparked by News Stories

Cryptic

News headline: "Cats' faces really are hard to read, but some people can do it, study finds"

Despite centuries of cohabitation,
humans still find it hard to read a cat's mind,
let alone their face. A news article provides
a quiz, so you can test your skills at interpreting
feline expressions, so I decide to try it,
in honor of a grey cat who adopted me

for a time. But I'm here to tell you,
the test is cryptic. My performance is dismal,
barely better than I might have achieved
flipping a coin, which makes me wonder,
what if it's really *cats* who are behind this little test,
and each time the link is clicked, they jostle

and cluster around a computer in some secluded lab,
eyes intent, tails twitching, as they watch the results
roll in. They stand on their hind legs, clad in
white jackets with their names embroidered
on the left chest, Bolt and Truffles
and Jinx and Emmitt, Mamba and Furball,

Ripley and Rogue, all the tabbies and calicos,
the Russian blues, the Persian long-hairs,
the Siamese, their faces inscrutable, because,
let's face it, if dogs are an open book,
cats are a cryptogram, a handful of zen koans,
the sound of a single hand clapping

an off-beat rhythm. When the window for the quiz
closes, the cats in the lab give each other high fives
(or, in the case of the polydactyls, high sixes)
as analysis confirms that we humans
don't understand them at all. Not even
a little bit. Mission accomplished.

The Truth Is Out
News headline: "Cats classified as 'invasive alien species' by Polish institute"

The truth is out at last,
slipping into the public consciousness
like a crafty feline might squeeze
past its keeper's legs to seek
the wider world.

Someone finally said it: cats are
an *alien species*, and furthermore,
invasive. Many questions remain, including,
when did their ships arrive, and
which

of the night sky's brilliant pinpricks
represents the sun of their home system,
but these are small matters,
inconsequential, really, compared
to the reality of our situation.

It's too late, now, for the finest
military minds to determine
a defensive strategy—the invaders
have infiltrated our society
purrfectly.

Now, as we do our best to ignore
the reproachful glares of our canine
companions—*we tried to warn you,
we really did*—there is only one
thing

to do. Given that the truth
is out, the next move
is up to them. We can only wait
to see what our feline overlords
have in mind
for us.

Hanging Them Up
*News headline: "Hamilton police service dog
Scout retires after nearly seven years"*

There comes an end to all trails,
no matter how savory, how hot
the scent. Newly retired—
do you understand the term?—
you might well gnaw at the problem
of why your human partner leaves
for shift without you, now; wonder
whether you, who have always tried
so hard to please, have unwittingly
committed some transgression
that cuts you from the chase.

We who have retired already,
we who have looked over the pasture
fence more than once wondering
what the rest of the herd was up to,
understand how hard it hits when
the time comes to hang up the badge,
hand in the ID tag. Still, nobody wants
to be like the athlete who hangs on
a season too long, hung out to dry
like a baserunner caught in a rundown
between third and home. There is no
shame in calling it a day.

Take pride instead, in the knowledge
that for a time, you
had a nose for the job, finding suspects
in unlikely places, recovering
ill-gotten goods, tracking the lost,
the wanderers, before the body
as well as the trail grew cold. Stories
for a grey-muzzled elder to tell the pups
in front of the fire on a winter day.

Chaser Checks Out
News headline: "Chaser, the border collie that could recognize more than 1,000 words, has died"

Chaser checked out, July 2019,
after a life spent in pursuit
of learning, her master,
a psychology professor,
having taught her words
for over 1,022 objects

a border collie,
Chaser's eagerness for work
lay keen as her steely gaze,
and so she mastered them all,
all the names for her individual toys—
two dozen-plus fetch discs,
over a hundred balls,
800 stuffed animals,
and sundry other items, too—

nouns buried
in her subconscious
like savory bones
with a subtle mental map
to find and bind them all

the language of love
she knew as well; barked a farewell
to her master, hours before he passed,
and perhaps, somewhere, they're
reunited now; he talking, she cocking
her head, as they count out with joy,
with feeling, the long, long litany of words
he taught, she learned

Lost and Found
News headline: "Tennessee Couple Finds Stray Dog Cuddled Up Next To Them In Bed"

a storm, and open door,
a hairy Houdini,
chains of coincidences
can fall like dominoes—
if it weren't for this, or that
we might be anywhere

and so it happened
that a couple who figured
the third warm body
joining them in bed one night
was one of their own three canines
turned out to be wrong

ah, the way our assumptions
have a way of staring us in the face
the next morning—

the light of dawn confirmed
that a neighbour's Lab-bulldog mix
had sauntered into the couple's house
to make herself at home
in their bed

not all who wander are lost
or must remain so,
not all incursions into our personal
space are unfriendly,
or intended to be

the dog was eventually reunited
with her people, and the rest of us
have reason to hope
that even if we find ourselves
in the wrong place, some day,
we might yet see a happy ending

Military Ghost Dog
News headline: "Ghost Robotics
now makes a lethal robot dog"

the milit'ry ghost dog's a marvelous chap
with sensors instead of a snout,
his vision can survey 360 degrees—
he's handy when used as a scout

for training, you don't have to ply him with treats
his tradecraft is learned through programming
the data collected gets sent to his handler
as long as there's no signal-jamming

you can send him to deal with explosives and bombs
though you may never see him again
you don't need to bathe him, he won't roll in ick,
he can master the roughest terrain

he's doesn't have fur for soft pats and ear scratches,
he isn't the greatest to cuddle
but there's one thing to say in the ghost dog's defense:
you won't need to clean up his puddles

For Laika
(The First Dog in Space)

all those days, those cold and lonely nights, a stray
scrounging for food through Moscow's lean streets
enduring the booted foot, the cast stone, the winter wind's
bitter bite you never sought to fly so high

those who found you had other ideas
and it must have seemed pleasant, at first
to have so much attention —
the photos snapped before Sputnik 2's launch
show your face, open-mouthed and eager,
up-pricked ears bearing a jaunty forward tilt
as though you couldn't wait to set your feet
on adventure's bright path

after blast-off, when you felt
the press of gravity's iron paw
and heard the rockets howling
like some relentless predator
racing in pursuit
it must have made your previous tribulations seem
trivial

it's said that over-heating
caused you to succumb to death's light embrace
after your capsule completed
a few circuits of the Earth

perhaps that's just as well —
this was, by design, a one-way voyage

alone, at the end, did you regret
you never had the chance to tell them
you'd have happily settled
for a good long car ride
with your head thrust out an open window?

*Laika, a stray dog launched into space on Sputnik 2 in November, 1957, was the first living creature to orbit the Earth.

Coda and Laika in Space

The Cats Have Their Say

*A response, from a feline viewpoint,
to the previous poem*

Are we not cats? Are we not splendid?
Then why do humans
show such favoritism
toward our canine cousins?

Take military ghost dogs. *Yes. Please do.*
Why use *dogs* as the template
for wonder weapons,
and not cats?

Consider our virtues.
We love to patrol at night,
but during times of non-action,
are only too happy to sleep.
And the thought of a spectral cat
leaping from the heights, unexpected—
does this not terrify you?

We are stealth. We are cunning.
We pad on noiseless feet.
And as for military strategy,
we could master that
in our sleep.

We can go undercover as house pets,
as we have so often before.
        Wait! You're not supposed to know that.
We will do everything you ask of us
we promise. *With metaphorical fingers crossed.*

Are we not cats? Are we not splendid?
Then why not use *us*
as the blueprint for military ghost creatures?
We would be perfection, indeed—
as long you don't ask us
to climb backwards down a tree.

Canem Roboto

News headline: "Robotic dogs and fish could help explore deeper into other worlds"

Day 1: Ace, Bravo, and Captain disembark from the autonomous lander, mechanical paws stirring the turquoise Martian dust. They are ready to travel where wheeled rovers cannot go. To sniff out new information. To explore heretofore unseen territory. Though tentative at first, they find their footing, revelling in the lighter gravity.

> bounding the dunes—
> each day
> a fresh adventure

Day 10: Back on Earth, NASA continues to share images captured by the canid robots. Everyone is amazed. Everyone except for the cats, that is. Felines hold a protest outside NASA headquarters, complaining loudly. Their argument comes down to this: You should have modelled the robots after us. We are programmed for curiosity, and we always land on our feet.

> dearer than catnip—
> thrill of exploring
> new spaces

Scientists hide their smiles. Cats were, indeed, considered as a model for the new exploration robots. But who needs a mechanical device with attitude? One that demands 20 hours of sleep a day and is predisposed to do as it pleases, rather than what *you* please?

Day 340: Puppyish enthusiasm gone, the robot dogs are all business. Loyal to their cause, they patrol their new planet. Day after twenty-four-plus-hour day. Dutiful. Tireless.

Still, they can't help but notice how the eternal cold gets in their joints.

> temperature check at Martian poles—
> a three-dog night
> indeed

Day 365: Back on Earth, the techs run diagnostics, remotely.

> system downtime—
> they dream of chasing rabbits
> under orange skies

Day 3,650: Human colonists arrive at last.

> fin-down at sunset—
> fierce joy
> of reunion

Day 7,000: The colonists have kept the canids running as long as possible, but Martian dust is a formidable enemy. Besides, with the cost of shipping goods from Earth, spare parts are more valuable than gold, almost as precious as oxygen.

The assigned tech flips the off switch, quelling forever the glow from those eerie eyes. With sure and steady hands, he dismantles each canid, one by one. Just doing his job.

Still, he is never the same, afterwards. There is something about the companionship of two legs and four that is ingrained in the human psyche. It feels wrong, somehow, what he's done.

Had he asked, Ace and the others would have told him not to worry. Told him that there is no fault in mercy. In providing dignity at the end.

> to everything its time—
> called home
> like all good dogs

Legendary:
Riffing on Myth, Legend, and Folklore

From Cat to Fiddle

do you remember
that magical night—
the laughing, leaping cow
kicking her heels high
over the moon—

the dog couldn't stop
laughing, while you and I
played a merry tune,
a down-east jig,
the dish and the spoon
spinning and whirling
across the green,
dancing till dawn

but dish and spoon
slipped away and left us,
no forwarding address,
left us in the stark light
of morning-after, cow
nursing a sore leg
from a rough landing,
dog holding her aching sides—

if only we had known, then,
that good times don't last
and the gang won't all be here
forever and a day like we imagined
once upon a golden moon
once upon a time

Nursery Rhymes for Changing Times

cupboards empty again—
Mother Hubbard's dog
orders biscuits online

exterminator's visit just completed—
visiting cat pursues
the Queen's computer mouse

video of fiddling cat
draws millions of likes—
dish and spoon regret departure

Midnight

What <u>Really</u> Happened
*Inspired by Eugene Field's
"The Duel"*

only the Border Collie knows
what *really* happened
in the matter of
Gingham v. Calico
and she's not telling

as for witness testimony—
that old clock, he'd say anything
to save face
and you know how the plate
loves to *dish*

no-one investigated the crime scene
the way they do on *NCIS* or *CSI*—
scraps of fabric
stuffed under the chair
never got sent to the Lab
who might have sniffed out
tell-tale DNA—a perfect match
to other unsolved capers
(the disappearing duck-boot,
the missing mock-neck)

only the Border Collie knows
what *really* happened
to Gingham and Calico
and she's not telling

*Wait! Is that a pig's ear?
And a marrow bone?*

"Pull up a chair,"
she says with a knowing wink.
"I'll give you the real story."

Thoughts on Cerberus

If two heads are better than one
then three must reign supreme—
take Cerberus, Hades' hound,
charged with devouring would-be escapees

and repelling living humans from the gates
of Hell. Three snouts to warn of pending danger,
six ears to hear the stealthiest of treads,
six eyes to fix upon unwelcome strangers—

this Cerberus is a wondrous beast, indeed!
As a dog owner myself, I know it must be hard;
three sets of teeth to brush—pet dental bills
are horrors worthy of the place that Cerby guards—

three bowls to fill and clean,
six ears to scratch behind—
Which makes me wonder,
how *does* his master ever find the time?

Musings of a Shelter Dog

In legend, my kind recalls the birth of First Dog
The wolf who turned from the comfort of the pack
To join the furless, dull-toothed tribe of man
Amid the painted walls of a smoky cave.
Lured by promises of warmth and kindness
He did not think of sadness or regret.

Once his paws had trod that road, too late for regret
Turning slowly from wild wolf to dog
He wagged his tail at any sign of kindness,
Accepted humans as his new-found pack.
Seeking shelter from howl of wind in caves
He huddled close to warming fires of man.

Not always kind, though, is this thing called "man"
The shelters teem with those who might regret
The first dog's foray into the first cave
And when your kind is unkind to we dogs
We hear in our hearts the call of the ancient pack
And chew on broken promises of kindness.

When does one learn cruelty or kindness?
You cannot wait till boy turns into man.
Like wolves, you must teach the youth of the pack
If you would avert the need for regret.
Oh, teach them to be kind to man and dog
Or you are no better than when you lived in caves.

Here at the shelter, I'm locked in a wire cave.
Humans has rarely ever shown me kindness.
It makes me wonder why you called First Dog
To join you by your fire, ancient man.
Far too late now, though, despite regret
Too late for us to join the wild pack.

For your pack, however cruel, is now our pack,
Your cave, however cold, is now our cave.
Turning from the howling winds of regret
We yearn to lap from the river of human kindness.
Oh, strive to be worthy of the title "Man,"
And act in ways that earn the love of dog.

Don't make us regret leaving the ancient pack.
Remember First Dog in the first stone cave,
And the promise of kindness given by First Man.

Spacy Gracie

The Last Dog

For countless many years of the earth's passage around the sun, people and dogs lived in symbiotic harmony. They walked together. They played together. They worked together. Life was, inarguably, good for both species. And if, from time to time, human noticed their dogs cocking their heads, as though listening to a distant music carried on the breeze, they thought little of it.

But change is constant, particularly when humans are involved. Life's pace became more and more frenetic, as though humans sought to cram as much as they could into the years and months and days allotted to them. Greedy as dogs wolfing their food, they sought to devour as much of life as they could. Faster, faster. Sidewalks were commandeered by speed-pods ferrying kids to school or adults to work or adults to appointments and commitments and entertainment. The ubiquitous delivery carts added to the hazards of the daily walk. Most simply gave it up. Playtimes, too, shortened, then stopped as humans became obsessed with their own affairs.

Breeders were the first to notice when the litters became smaller and smaller, and finally females stopped whelping. But what was the big deal? Demand for pets was plummeting faster than real estate stocks in a recession. *Why not adopt?* people said smugly. Good advice, in any era. But even the shelters grew empty.

The last dog known to live with a human was a grey-muzzled old girl, much loved. The day her owner passed away, she slipped out into the night, never to be seen again on this planet. But a neighborhood security camera, had anyone cared to look, captured an image. A head, lifting, as though alert to a distant music that still played, had always played, in the distance. A tail, beginning to wag, as understanding dawned.

> door to a different dimension—
> she turns three times
> then disappears

The Great Hereafter

The Cat's Message

breeze wafts through open window
small creatures squeak in the grass
and a moonbeam begins a slow march
across the living room floor

you snore, still, in bed,
and I wonder at the fact
that you cannot hear the full moon's call
as it casts its silver gleam across the lawn

do not scold me when I waken you
asking to be let out—
evening's hours, like all our hours,
are short and bear their numbers

I glance at your face, as you sway,
eyes heavy with sleep, to grumblingly hold
the door ajar—

do not fear, I will be back
and if not, do not lament
I live life on my own terms
and the mice await

To Let You Go Gently

To all things come an end, it's said
but I am not yet ready to surrender
your soul to that cold night.
Part of me prays
that you won't want to leave us, too soon,
but I know it's a kind of selfishness
as I watch your painful step
and see you labor to move stiff joints in the morning,
so I give thanks for every day
that you show the joy of life still—
rolling and scrubbing in the backyard grass,
barking at your buddies,
brandishing one of your well-worn chew-toys
with that old-time grin,
and I pray to the higher power
to grant me, when That Time arrives,
the courage to look in your eyes
and read truly what is written there
and to let you go gently
when it's time.

Farewell to an Old Friend

I can still remember the moment I knew with certainty that the day was drawing near.

I was walking the dogs in the shiver of a pre-dawn morning when I saw a meteor slowly, almost lazily, etching a silver trail across the sky. I knew from meteor and the frost on the fallen leaves, the frost that matched the whiteness spreading across her muzzle and her face, that the time for farewells was approaching.

Considering I had a year's warning, I should have been ready.

But of course I was not.
***
It seems a shabby way to say goodbye to an old and most dear friend, tossing dirt over a sheet-wrapped husk that once was home to a loyal heart, and I wonder where she is now; whether she has crossed that bridge of many colours; whether she will chase the golden sun across the sky as if it were nothing more than a giant tennis ball tossed by the gods for her amusement; whether somewhere, somehow her soul is entering the body of a newborn border collie pup about to take its first gasping breaths.
***
Later, I will take solace in the photos that show how gaunt she had become, how her eyes were misted with pain. But for now, there is only guilt and sadness for the quickness of the passing years, the unappreciated times that have flowed, irretrievably, down that river we can never step in quite the same way again, no matter how we might long to do so.

> bare branches, grey sky
> and the honking
> of a solitary goose

The Only Enduring Thing

All through the morning, the maples weep yellow tears. Fallen leaves form a gilded carpet in the woods, providing brightness on a day burdened with sorrow.

In a small natural clearing, I carefully place several rocks patterned with the fossil remains of past sea creatures, using them to mark the boundaries of my border collie Sneeks' final resting spot. Weighted by age, the fossilized rocks strike me as a fitting symbol of the mystery of love, which in the end is the only enduring thing.

Next, I plant flower bulbs over the spot where she lies, beauty as a protest against the winter that comes for all living things. Through the long snows that follow, the bulbs slumber. But in springtime, around Easter, greenery comes to life, pushing through the earth to seek the sun.

>   daffodils bloom—
>   after winter's darkness
>   light prevails

Paws for Reflection

my two dogs proved
to be clumsy gardeners—
their boisterous game of chase
taking them careening
through the unfenced vegetable garden

where they romped through the radishes
and pranced through the peas,
trampled the tomatoes
and bounded through the beans,
then pirouetted in the pepper patch
for good measure

soil churned and turned
to their satisfaction
they flopped in the grass, panting,
and grinned as if to say,
"there, we aerated the soil—
no need to thank us"

that year's ravaged crops
are long gone
the dogs, too, buried
having lived to an old age
but what wouldn't I give
for one more chance to watch them
romp through the radishes,
prance through the peas

Now You're Gone

You didn't always bark when they passed,
the other people with their canine companions,
strolling down the sidewalk in front of our house.

Selective, you were, giving voice when you saw
some dogs but not others; maybe you thought
you recognized a friend and called out, but when

they turned around you realized you were mistaken
and that's okay. If we live long enough,
we all step into the stream of loss, sooner or later.

I look out the window and remember how car noises
scared you, and strangers, and thunderstorms,
and unfamiliar places; my fault, really,

I should have exposed you to more, as a pup.
Still, I can't complain about the time we spent
together. Just that it was too short and I'm left

to sit at my desk and watch the people
walking their dogs as they pass
on my own, now that you're gone.

Without Her

hands my dog once kept busy
with so many morning rituals—
walks, feeding, brushing—
now sit idle, unsure

how to occupy themselves,
and the laziness of knowing
I'm no longer on call
for nature's call

doesn't feel like a luxury—
I'm left behind, bereft,
like an unpaired sock,
salt without pepper,

Laurel minus Hardy,
left to wonder whether
the early-morning birds
still sing as loud without us

there to listen; whether
twilight bats still zip
and dip across the evening sky
without us there to see

Herding the Stars

You run way ahead and you chase tennis balls
You bark at the squirrels and you climb up the walls
You've got energy to spare
Is there ever a moment of peace, anywhere?

The time's drawing nearer, quickly
When this stage of my youth morphs to dim memory

When I'm watching TV now you doze at my feet
Or lie by the wood stove to soak up the heat
On our walks, you're at my side
Not running ahead, but just matching my stride

I am calmer, but still you must know
I am ready to follow wherever you go

Here's your leash, for a walk—do you still want to, though,
Now your leg joints are stiff and your pace is so slow?
Say, where is that dog who once used to run,
Outpacing the breeze as though shot from a gun?

Hold fast to your memories
Of the rambunctious pup that I once used to be

The time has now come—as we knew—we must part
And I feel like I've carved out a piece of my heart
You have wandered off so far
Are you chasing the moonbeams and herding the stars?

Look in your heart and believe
I'll be right there beside you when you think of me.

Over the Rainbow

I
I've long clung fast to the story
about the rainbow bridge, and the meadow
where our furry friends of bygone years await,
but the passing of my border collie
in cold and gloomy February hit me
harder than expected and afterward, I,
having passed the threshold of sixty years
on this blue planet, could suddenly glimpse
that indistinct and distant shore that lies ahead,
knew for certain I was headed there as well

II
so easy to say, *we'll cross that bridge
when we come to it,* then
push all thought from our minds
like we tend to do with unappealing
notions. Like spiders. Or death.
Or our own mortality. We try
to forget, until some loss
comes along to remind us.

III
it's said that a cat doesn't just purr when it's happy,
but also when it wishes to comfort itself,
and maybe stories like the rainbow bridge
are the same thing, an expression
of our deepest yearnings, told over
and over as though repetition
might make them more real

IV
then again, maybe stories are a place
where deeper truths reside

V
not everything that is true can be
explained, and not every explanation
encompasses what's important.
Take a rainbow, for example.
You can talk about reflection and
refraction and dispersion, but those words
don't capture the magic.
The catch of breath at the beauty.
There's more to life than facts. Formulas.
Objects that can be touched and seen.
So I will choose to cling to hope,
and believe in that story that tells us
they are there, in that vast and grassy
meadow, all the beloved pets
who left us too soon, eyes alert, heads
high, waiting for us to arrive
so we can cross that bridge together.

Here/Not Here

she is here, and not here,
my old dog—
the radio station
plays the songs I heard
as her health declined

memories
intertwine with music—
silken ears, a laughing smile,
the weight of her nose
on my knee—

Ravioli

The Unknown After

I
late May—
we bury our old dog's remains
under two young saplings

the weight
of that bag of ashes
when I carry it out to the yard—

there's a heaviness to guilt
and second-guessing,
to the not-knowing
whether you chose the right time
to say goodbye

II
November snowfall—
the oak still clings to her leaves
as though she, too,
finds it hard
to let go

III
December twilight—
mourning doves
call from the cedars

IV
early March—
snow on the ground,
patchy

a skein of northbound geese,
loose-strung, spans across the sky

proclaiming, as they go,
that we all must trace our path one day
into the unknown after

Ghostly Dog

you are passing familiar, ghostly dog,
though your shape is insubstantial
that greying snout, that furrowed brow,
that white-tipped tail, that playful bow
I feel that I should know you

what is your nature, ghostly dog?
you race through the leaves, yet make no sound
dig in the dirt without raising a mound
you can guess, I am sure, if you open your mind
I am the One who can't leave you behind

where might I find you, ghostly dog?
look on the trails that we walked in the fall
under the shrub where I hid with my ball
padding behind you along silent halls
of the house we shared together

when will I see you, ghostly dog?
come, now, no need to hasten that day
be happy to know that we once shared space
allow me to visit, to gaze at your face
till the day comes that we're reunited

This Tree

This tree is part dog
though its bark is silent.
My border collie's ashes
rest beneath its roots.

Some days,
its leaves quiver,
restless as hounds
before a hunt.

Some days, it basks
in summer's warmth,
like a dog, asprawl
in a patch of sunlight.

Branches sway
as I walk past,
tails wagging
a friendly greeting.

Ghost Train

There's a provincial park in Ontario where a train used to run, years ago. Rails forgotten now, long gone, but it's said you can hear the ghost train passing when the conditions are right, in the valley. Though I hiked the ghost train trail more than once with my dogs Sneeks and Jak, I can't say I ever heard it.

>   wind through the trees—
>   we tread the bottom
>   of an ancient sea

Still, the dogs loved that path. Sneeks would often let loose a yelp of sheer delight when we arrived at the parking lot.

Years have flown by. Sneeks and Jak have passed on, and I've moved to a different part of the province. Still, I yearn to go back and walk that trail once more, even though I know these kinds of experiences can never be the same, because we have changed, and the trees have changed, and we carry with us all the other selves we have been in the interim.

My ears have become less sharp with time. As though to compensate, my heart hears things it was deaf to before. I've come to think that there is a ghost train inside of all of us, and it sings longer and louder as we age, and more and more of those we once loved leave us behind, moving onto the next dimension, wherever that might be.

>   autumn afternoon hike—
>   around a bend we seek
>   glimpses of old ghosts

It's hard to resist the temptation to set our feet on roads we've walked before, hoping to seize a piece of the past, to trick ourselves into believing those we loved are still here, or that our innocent selves are still as they once were. But isn't that what memory is all about, binding and weaving yesterday to today, so that we might spin out toward tomorrow with hopeful hearts?

> I stand on the ridge—
> in the distance
> a happy woof

Ghost Dogs at Play

ghost dogs at play
with a laughing look on each face
ghost dogs at play
with a yip, a yap, and a bay
round the house and the yard they race
in a fleet-footed game of chase
ghost dogs at play

> sunlight refracts
> through tears of joy—
> rainbow bridge

Cats and Dogs
of the Future

The Changing Face of Fear

Hallowe'en night 2060—
at the door, an alien
bares its fangs

she laughs—
is that supposed to scare me?
take your treats and go

what she really fears—
in the living room
her teething puppy

The 22nd Century Guide to Purr-sonality Types
Excerpted from HR Today, July, 2120

Forget the old labels, throw them out.
Blues and Green and Orange. Directing
and Calculating. Where did the previous
personality philosophies get us?
Cities full of smoking holes where
houses used to be. And gen-mods,

lots of them, at the cellular level, thanks to the rads.
Today's law-of-the-jungle business world
calls for more of an animal flair. Dog people,
of course, are easy to pick out. Loyal. Team players.
But they don't really think for themselves,
if you know what I mean. Now cat people,

they're a different story. Cryptic and self-serving,
but smart enough to know when they need to collaborate.
They're the ones you see sitting in the corners
at business meetings, waiting to pounce
on someone else's mistake. Sharpening their claws
at performance review time. Preening when they think

nobody's looking. How to know
if you have a plethora of cat people?
Check out the cafeteria's sales trends
for fish Fridays. And there are other clues.
Shredded memos in the copy room,
when you know the shredding machine

has been broken for months.
The purr of self-satisfaction in their voices
when they know they're right.
Which, in their view, is, like, all the time.
The way you don't have problems finding volunteers
for the midnight shift. The fact that

you haven't had to call the exterminator
for months, because you don't have a rodent
problem anymore. Not even a rodent opportunity.
And if you're still in doubt, take the ones you suspect out
for pizza night. If their three-topping personal
pizza comes back with anchovies, anchovies, anchovies,

you've got your man. Or woman. Meaning, cat.
But it could be worse. Snake people
can't be trusted. Horse people
pull their weight, but can't seem to shake
that flight instinct. Cat people really are
the cat's meow. And they won't let you forget it.

The Cats of the Future

the cats of the future
will come in many colors—
green tabbies, rainbow calicos,
Russian blues in fifty
shades of grey

the cats of the future
will fearlessly tread
in the pawprints of Félicette,
first feline in space,
though hoping for a gentler fate

the cats of the future
will sharpen their claws
on artificial trees, maintaining morale
on space-bound colony ships,
because wherever humans go

the cats of the future
will follow, and wherever
cats go, they'll do their level best
to keep the dogs of the future
in their place

Dogs of the 2080s

mission to Titan—
robot dog
fetches data

online catalogue—
they deliberate over options
for gene-spliced designer dogs

K-9 expansion pack—
dogs and owners hike
through virtual worlds

canine deity
tramples his bed
spiral galaxy

alternate reality—
uplifted dogs
clone their favorite humans

Chimerapet

merino retriever—
watchdog with golden fleece
a crafter's dream

pot-bellied pig dog—
ah, the clatter of hooves
on Christmas morning . . .

Siamese cat-bird—
which came first
the kitten or the egg?

Canis Futuris

perhaps
there is such a thing
as too much authenticity—
the android dog
steals her sandwich

six legs and two heads—
and *what* is that *smell?*
the colonists stare
at the alien creature
the dog carted home.

programming glitch—
robot dog chases
its tail
its tail
its tail

Dogs in Space

thirty-five-year mission—
to find new worlds
to mark as their own

diplomatic faux pas—
if only the aliens' ship
hadn't looked like a fetch toy

sentient flora—
a whole new significance
to barking up the wrong tree

puppy gets a scolding—
so hard to resist chasing
the ship's cat

Fidelis Reinvented

"Look, Mom," Nessie says
and her mother Tashu turns to watch
as Nessie teaches her candroid dog
a new trick

unbidden, a memory:
Tashu tossing the tennis ball
for her German Shepherd Tuffy
his feet pounding across the grass —
real grass —

of course, Tashu tells herself,
real dogs have their drawbacks
and she smiles as she remembers
the spit-soaked ball
the pong of wet fur
the mucky paws

besides, there's not much space
for dogs to run
on a colony ship

she feels a stab of fear
as she wonders,
*will it really be better
where we're going?*

"Shake," Nessie says

as the candroid lifts its left forepaw
and places it in the girl's hand
Tashu nods encouragement
through a haze of tears

When We Leave Home for Good

In the eerie silence
that follows the Final Pandemic
and its attendant misfortunes,
how long will it take

for the small creatures—
the mice, the scolding squirrels,
the cheek-packed chipmunks—
to find the cracks, the gaps,

the vulnerable spots to push against
as they move into our houses,
seeking shelter against
the indifferent winter?

Snow will fall, as it did before,
though there is no one to clear it
from the concrete sidewalk
where chattering high schoolers

used to pass, never seeming to be
dressed warmly enough against
the east wind's bite, for fear
of not looking cool.

Grass will grow knee-tall,
rhubarb and asparagus will run wild,
and shy deer will come to graze
the apple tree's tender branches.

Oh, the cat might
miss us for awhile,
complaining when he finds
the food bowl empty,

but he'll remember soon enough
how to fend for himself
and the dogs may mourn
our absence for a space,

till they form their own packs
and gallop through the fields, barking
at the moon or at nothing at all
with no-one to tell them "no."

The Sand Dogs of Mars

for six months, life on these red sands seemed bland,
all study and rigor and rules and strict compliance—
and then we discovered them, muzzles to the stars
and singing, the sand dogs of Mars

at first, we didn't credit the witness of our eyes,
imagined it wishful thinking for those we left behind
all the Fidos and Rexes and Maxes and Milos and Bandits
but then we felt that coarse fur under our gloved hands

for now, they will remain our tight-kept secret
Mission Control, we fear, won't understand
might compel us to sacrifice our new friends on the altars
of science, so for now, this is our small act of defiance

we've bitten the apple of knowledge, cannot deny
that wonders exist beneath these yellow-brown skies
so close we might touch them with our gloved hands
here among the redness of the sands

beautiful mysteries under the sky-bright stars—
the sand dogs of Mars

Steampunk Paradise

In the halls of Steampunk Paradise,
steampunk cats chase steampunk mice
while steampunk dogs with dented ears
go leaping after steampunk deer
until their humans call them in
and scratch behind their ears of tin.
They rest their heads on masters' knees
engaging in deep reveries;
a heartfelt sigh, a steamy hiss,
convey the depths of canine bliss
then lids drop over glowing eyes
in the halls of Steampunk Paradise.

A Cat's Confession

Forgive me, master, for I have sinned—
I know you hate it when I capture birds
but that black-capped chickadee at the feeder,
I honestly thought his reflexes would be quicker.
You know what they say.
Survival of the fittest.

Forgive me, master, for I have sinned—
I smacked the dog in the nose again.
It was her fault. She keeps trying to herd me.
Besides, her breath stinks
and she doesn't even know how to use a litter box.
I have no idea why you keep her around.

Forgive me, master, for I have sinned—
I sharpened my claws on the couch. Many times.
Perhaps you can take it back and get a new one.
I prefer a fabric with a thicker nap, myself.

For these my sins, I offer
my most insincere remorse.

Then again, you let the kibble level
fall to calamitous levels the other day
(I actually saw the bottom of my dish!)
so I consider us even.

Now, if you would be so good
as to let me out—

Separate and Apart

Two generations after the Big Bang—
the atomic one, not the formation-of-the-universe one—
First Cat ascended to the leadership

and he gathered those of us who had Changed,
in the years since, and who now wore a different guise.
And we sat, with our triangular ears up-pricked,

our whiskers bristling, our tails twitching,
as the sun beamed down through the leaves of a surviving maple.
And First Cat said, "We are new and different,

separate and apart. We may be descended from humans,
but we will not walk in the old paths, follow the old ways.
It behooves us to create a new mythology to frame our experience.

This will be our First Task." And so the greatest minds
among the Cat People turned their thoughts
to explaining the world through new eyes. It was, in truth,

a welcome distraction from lean rations and tainted water.
And we created tales of a feline deity, Magnus Cattus,
who carved the riverbeds with a sandpaper tongue,

and who used his giant forepaws to bat the Earth around the sun
which itself is a giant flaming hairball that will one day burn out,
thought hopefully not soon. And we re-invented the constellations—

the yarn ball, the scratching post, the milk pitcher.
The Swashbuckling Cat, with his three-star sword.
And First Cat purred, and said, "It is well."

And he reminded us, "We are different from the humans who came before." And he prepared to introduce the Second Task.
We leaned forward, exchanging glances, eager for his words.

What *would* be next? To invent space flight,
to carry us from this cursed rock? To institute medical training,
so the mortality rate among our young might be improved?

But no. The Second Task was to prepare for warfare against the Dog People. And it came to me then, though I dared not speak it—
perhaps we had not travelled so far from human after all.

An Understanding

under Fenmor's green skies
the explorers gaze upward
dwarfed by the twin statues
the only artifacts
left standing

around them
building blocks lie scattered
destruction wrought by weapons
as far beyond their comprehension
as algebra is, to an infant

their jaws sagging, just a little—
for they didn't expect *this*—
they gaze at the inscrutable faces
the eyes set with emeralds
glittering green against the grey

ah, what these hands hath wrought

but those arms are not truncated
by hands and fingers, but rather—

they capture the image on their screens

when they send their report, no need
to add explanatory text, though they think it:

at last we understand the origin
of the saying
curiosity killed the cat

"What's got into *him*?"
the Captain just shrugs—
ship's cat stalks his prey
across strange dimensions
beyond human ken.

Unexpected

first day on Deneb IV—
on the way back to camp,
a large grey cat-wolf
intercepts the explorers

bristling and baring her teeth
she blocks the path
till someone stops
to pat her

a swim in Arcadia's murky river
paints each of her hairs
with fluorescent motes—
outside the cabin, our dog
shimmers in the twilight

playing fetch on Mars—
my border collie
more tireless than ever

References for "From the Headlines" Poems

Several poems in the "From the Headlines" chapter were sparked by news articles. Below is a list of the relevant articles, listed by alphabetical order of the poem in question. Though links were verified at the time of manuscript drafting, they may have since changed.

"Canem Roboto"
MacDonald, Bob. "Robotic dogs and fish could help explore deeper into other worlds." *cbc.ca/radio.* Posted January 15, 2021. Accessed January 17, 2021.
https://www.cbc.ca/radio/quirks/robotic-dogs-and-fish-could-help-explore-deeper-into-other-worlds-1.5875143

"Chaser Checks Out"
"Chaser, the border collie that could recognize more than 1,000 words, has died." *As It Happens, cbc.ca.* Posted July 30, 2019. Accessed August 1, 2019.
https://www.cbc.ca/radio/asithappens/as-it-happens-tuesday-edition-1.5230248/chaser-the-border-collie-that-could-recognize-more-than-1-000-words-has-died-1.5230263

"Cryptic"
Weber, Bob. "Cats' faces really are hard to read, but some people can do it, study finds." *cbc.ca.* Posted December 3, 2019. Accessed December 3, 2019. Link:
https://www.cbc.ca/news/science/cat-facial-expressions-1.5382018

"Hanging Them Up"
"Hamilton police service dog Scout retires after nearly seven years." *thespec.com.* Posted January 9, 2020. Accessed January 13, 2020.
https://www.thespec.com/news/hamilton-region/2020/01/09/hamilton-police-service-dog-scout-retires-after-nearly-seven-years.html

"Lost and Found"
Papenfuss, Mary. Tennessee Couple Finds Stray Dog Cuddled Up Next To Them In Bed." *yahoo.com*. Posted May 17, 2022. Downloaded May 18, 2022.
https://sports.yahoo.com/tennessee-couple-finds-stray-dog-084916702.html

"Military Ghost Dog"
Atherton, Kelsey D. "Ghost Robotics now makes a lethal robot dog." *popsci.com*. Posted October 13, 2021. Accessed October 14, 2021.
https://www.popsci.com/technology/ghost-robotics-robot-dog-gun-lethal/

"The Truth is Out"
Gera, Vanessa. "Cats classified as 'invasive alien species' by Polish institute." *cbc.ca*. Posted July 26, 2022. Accessed July 26, 2022.
https://www.cbc.ca/news/science/house-cats-invasive-species-polish-institute-1.6532330

Previous Appearances

Poems in this collection first appeared in the following publications (any omissions are unintentional). Alterations to wording or, in some cases, format, may have been made since original publication.

"Canem Roboto," *NewMyths,* Issue 55, June 2021.

[canine deity], *Spaceports and Spidersilk,* June 2022.

"Canis Futuris," *Eccentric Orbits: An Anthology of Sci-Fi Poetry, Volume 2,* edited by Wendy Van Camp, Dimensionfold Publishing, 2021.

"A Cat's Confession," *From a Cat's View: An Anthology of Stories Told by Cats,* edited by Robin Praytor, Post-to-Print Publishers, LLC, 2018.

"Cats of the Future," *Utopia Science Fiction,* Volume IV, Issue 1, August/September 2022.

"The Cat's Message," originally titled "Moonlight," *From a Cat's View: An Anthology of Stories Told by Cats,* edited by Robin Praytor, Post-to-Print Publishers, LLC, 2018.

"The Changing Face of Fear," *Eccentric Orbits: An Anthology of Science Fiction Poetry, Volume 3,* edited by Wendy Van Camp, Dimensionfold Publishing, 2022.

"Chaser Checks Out," *In Days to Come,* by Lisa Timpf, Hiraeth Publishing, 2022.

"Chimerapet," *Scifaikuest* May 2023 online edition (poem in this collection is abridged from original).

"Cryptic," *Polar Borealis,* Issue 18, May 2021.

"Dogs of the 2080s," *Eccentric Orbits: An Anthology of Science Fiction Poetry, Volume 3,* edited by Wendy Van Camp, Dimensionfold Publishing, 2022.

"Dogs in Space," *Scifaikuest* February 2023 print, Hiraeth Publishing.

"Farewell to an Old Friend," *Contemporary Haibun Online*, Vol. 4, No. 4, December 2008. Also included in *A Trail That Twines: Reflections on Life and Nature*, by Lisa Timpf, 2009.

"Fidelis Reinvented," *NewMyths*, Issue 43, June 2018; also included in *Passages* anthology.

"For Laika," *Lynn River Review Vol. 3: Resonance, Renaissance*, 2018; also included in *House of Zolo's Journal of Speculative Literature, Volume 2,* 2020.

"From Cat to Fiddle," *NewMyths,* Issue 48, September 2019, also included in *NeoSapiens* anthology.

"Ghost Train," *NewMyths,* Issue 61, Winter 2022.

"Now You're Gone," *Samjoko,* Summer 2022.

"Nursery Rhymes for Changing Times," *Scifaikuest* August 2021 print, Hiraeth Publishing. Abbreviated from original.

"Over the Rainbow," *NewMyths,* Issue 56-57, Fall/Winter 2021.

"Paws for Reflection," *The Clumsy Gardener, Thema,* Vol. 32 No. 1 Summer 2020.

[playing fetch on Mars], *Scifaikuest,* August 2017 print issue, Alban Lake Publishing.

"The Sand Dogs of Mars," *Polar Starlight* Issue 12, November 2023.

"Separate and Apart," *Illumen*, Spring 2022, Hiraeth Publishing.

[sunlight refracts], *Scifaikuest,* May 2022 online, Hiraeth Publishing.

[a swim in Arcadia's river], *Scifaikuest,* November 2019 online, Hiraeth Publishing.

"To Let You Go Gently," *Dog Blessings: Poems, Prose, and Prayers Celebrating Our Relationship with Dogs,* edited by June Cotner, 2007; also included in re-issued version of *Dog Blessings* anthology, 2017.

"An Understanding," *The Martian Wave*, 2018, Nomadic Delirium Press.

"Unexpected," *Utopia Science Fiction*, Vol. IV, Issue 1, August/September 2022.

"What *Really* Happened," *NewMyths*, Issue 44, September 2018.

"When We Leave Home for Good," *Polar Starlight*, Issue 3, October 2021.

"Without Her," *Samjoko,* Summer 2022.

Acknowledgements

I'd like to thank all of the zine, anthology, and magazine editors who have published my poems over the years. The boost of seeing my work in print, whether on paper or online, motivated me to keep writing. I'd also like to give a shout-out to those who, though they didn't accept my work for publication, offered comments, either noting that one of the poems came close, or giving some input on why something didn't work for them. Everyone's time is precious, and giving some of it to an author when you don't have to is appreciated and makes a difference.

I'd also like to thank teachers, both in formal classrooms and online courses, who have helped me improve my skills, as well as Norfolk County's First Thursday Writers' Group, who, during the time I was a member, made some helpful suggestions about my writing projects.

About the Author

Lisa Timpf is a retired HR and communications professional who lives in Simcoe, Ontario. Lisa attended McMaster University in Hamilton, Ontario, where she obtained a Bachelor of Physical Education degree. She went on to study sport history at Dalhousie University in Halifax, Nova Scotia, taking courses at the Master's level but never quite getting her thesis past the third draft.

Lisa's poetry has appeared in *New Myths, Eye to the Telescope, Star*Line, Polar Borealis, Triangulation: Habitats,* and other venues. She has also had over 50 short stories and a number of creative non-fiction pieces published. Her interest in gardening, nature, the environment, and sports are often reflected in her writing.

Cats and dogs have played an important role in Lisa's life over the years. In addition to offering companionship, they have provided inspiration for stories, poems, and non-fiction pieces. Lisa's border collie Emma and Russian Blue cat Smokey served as models for her short story characters Pepper and Quicksilver. Smokey, Emma, Australian shepherd cross Jak, and mischievous border collie cross Sneeks inspired many of the poems in the "The Great Hereafter" section of *Cats and Dogs in Space.*

Check out Lisa's website, http://lisatimpf.blogspot.com/, for more information about her writing projects.

www.ingramcontent.com/pod-product-compliance
Lightning Source LLC
LaVergne TN
LVHW021304080526
838199LV00090B/6003